W9-CHA-328

WASHINGTON

Past and Present

Daniel E. Harmon

rosen publishing's
rosen central®

New York

Published in 2010 by The Rosen Publishing Group, Inc.
29 East 21st Street, New York, NY 10010

First Edition

Library of Congress Cataloging-in-Publication Data

Harmon, Daniel E.
Washington: past and present / Daniel E. Harmon.—1st ed.
    p. cm.—(The United States: past and present)
Includes bibliographical references and index.
ISBN-13: 978-1-4358-5295-2 (library binding)
ISBN-13: 978-1-4358-5588-5 (pbk)
ISBN-13: 978-1-4358-5589-2 (6 pack)
1. Washington (State)—Juvenile literature. I. Title.
F891.3.H37 2010
979.7—dc22

                                                            2008054236

Manufactured in the United States of America

On the cover: Top left: Construction of the Grand Coulee Dam. Top right: A breathtaking aerial view of the Palouse Hills in southeastern Washington State. Bottom: A dusky look across the Seattle skyline toward Mount Rainier.

Contents

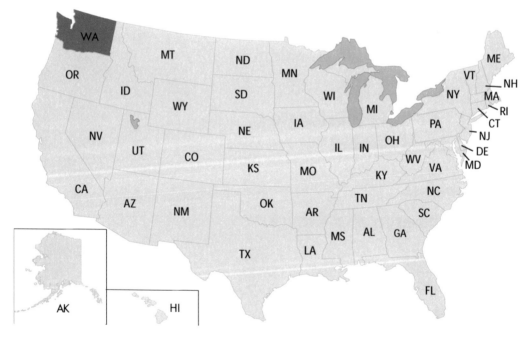

Washington is the northwestern-most state in the contiguous United States, bordered by Canada to the north, Idaho to the east, Oregon to the south, and the Pacific Ocean to the west.

Introduction

Washington is the only state named for a U.S. president. Just as George Washington was a fascinating man of many talents, the state is a fascinating place of many different faces and parts. It has rugged, majestic mountains; scenic, fish-filled rivers and lakes; a long Pacific coastline; towering forests; modern cities; and rolling farmland. Businesses of every sort thrive there, and Washingtonians from all cultures and walks of life love the state in which they live.

Washington was the northwestern corner of the United States for many years, until Alaska and Hawaii became states of the Union in 1959. Washington is a place of many faces, cultures, natural attractions, and adventures. It has been that way for a very long time.

Canada (British Columbia) is its northern neighbor. Oregon lies to the south, Idaho to the east. The Pacific Ocean washes its western shoreline. People on the opposite side of the Pacific have played major roles in Washington's progress, much like people across the Atlantic have shaped life in the East Coast states.

Washington is the nation's eighteenth-largest state and fifteenth-most-populated state. About six million people live on its 66,582 square miles (172,448 square kilometers) of land.

Washington's people, history, and importance to the nation are drawn from many sources and directions. From the tip of the famous Space Needle in Seattle to the highest mountain peaks, Washington is a state rich in heritage and natural treasures.

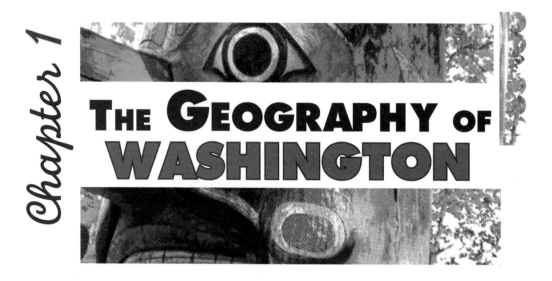

Chapter 1

THE GEOGRAPHY OF WASHINGTON

Washington is part of a region of the United States called the Pacific Northwest. Washington has six geographic areas:

- The Olympic Mountains cover the northwestern "shoulder" of the state. They lie south of the Strait of Juan de Fuca, between the Pacific Ocean and Puget Sound. Although not as high as some American mountain ranges, they form a rugged wilderness. Some parts of the Olympic Mountains have never been visited by humans.
- The Coast Range is the hilly region of the state's lower coastal area, extending into Oregon.
- The Puget Sound Lowlands are the land areas surrounding the great sound that reaches southward through western Washington. Partly because of its connection with the Pacific, the vicinity of the sound has become the most bustling and heavily populated part of the state.
- The Cascade Range dominates central Washington. These tall, ragged peaks rise in a wide band between the Oregon and British Columbia borders, east of Puget Sound. In the highest of the Cascades, snow covers the summits year-round.

A state-operated ferryboat crosses Puget Sound as the sun sets. In the background to the west are the Olympic Mountains, which lie between the sound and the ocean.

- The Columbia Plateau, or Columbia Basin, spans south-central and southeastern Washington. It was created thousands of years ago by melting lava that flowed from deep within the earth. The Columbia River, from which the plateau gets its name, and the Snake River run through this vast area.

- The long, high Rocky Mountain Range crosses the northeastern corner of the state. Washingtonians call this section of the Rockies the Columbia Mountains.

Natural Wonders, Natural Dangers

Fifty-seven people and countless animals were killed when Mount Saint Helens in southwestern Washington erupted May 18, 1980. Ash and smoke were blown 12 miles (19 km) into the sky at a speed of 650 miles per hour (1,046 km per hour)—the speed of a jet aircraft. Nearby towns were deep in ash, and the sky turned eerily dark. It was difficult to breathe. Ten million trees were blown over. In aerial photographs, they looked like scattered toothpicks. The eruption caused the most massive landslide ever recorded.

The volcano previously had erupted in 1837 and probably will again. Earthquakes, meanwhile, occur in the region much more frequently than volcanoes.

Throughout history, other kinds of tragedies have reminded Washington's people that along with natural beauty there is danger. Winter avalanches are not uncommon on the steep mountain slopes deep in snow. In February 1910, an avalanche derailed two trains that were stranded high in the Cascades between Spokane and Seattle. Ninety-six people died. Some were buried 40 feet (12 meters) beneath the snow.

The eruption of Mount Saint Helens in 1980 was among the most catastrophic natural events in U.S. history.

The geography of Washington provides two very different climates in the eastern and western parts of the state. Because western Washington is affected by the ocean, it is wetter and milder in climate than the eastern part of the state. Other wide ranges in climate are produced by the rain shadow effect of the Olympic Mountains. Quinault, located on Lake Quinault, receives as much as 137 inches (348 centimeters) of precipitation annually, whereas Sequim, only about 60 miles (97 km) north of it, can get less than 16 inches (41 cm) annually. The statewide annual average is about 46 inches (117 cm) of precipitation.

Rivers, Mountains, Sea, and Plateau

Washington is a mountainous state. Three notable mountain ranges cross or lie within its borders. Tall, aging trees—important to the state's economy—cover much of the mountain regions.

Washington's mountains are grand to see and explore. They can also be dangerous. The U.S. West Coast is part of what geologists call the Pacific Ring of Fire. This is the jagged, broken arc of landmasses extending from the southwestern Pacific Ocean northward to Alaska and down the coasts of the Americas. Most of the earth's active volcanoes lie along or inside the "ring."

Five Washington State mountains in the Cascade Range are volcanic. Four of them have erupted in the last two centuries. Most recently, Mount Saint Helens exploded in May 1980. It blew a great cloud of ash across the Northwest, settling as far off as Denver, Colorado.

The Rockies, the great system that extends from the American Southwest into Canada, loom above northeastern Washington. Through the center of the state, from Oregon to Canada, is the broad Cascade Range. It includes nationally famous peaks. Mount Rainier

Majestic Mount Rainier is one of the United States' highest peaks and is the highest in Washington State. The city in the foreground is Tacoma.

is the highest mountain in Washington and one of the highest in the United States (14,410 feet, or 4,392 meters). Near the coast, on the large peninsula between Puget Sound and the sea, are the smaller Olympic Mountains.

The Columbia is most prominent among the state's many rivers. It flows down from Canada through east-central Washington, then curves westward, forming much of the Washington-Oregon border. It empties into the Pacific.

The Okanogan also flows southward from Canada and joins the Columbia east of the Cascades. The Snake River, which begins in

Yellowstone National Park in Wyoming, joins the Columbia in southeastern Washington. This is in the area of the state known as the Columbia Plateau. The Columbia Plateau also covers parts of Idaho, Oregon, and Nevada. It is noted for its spacious wheat fields. Interestingly, beneath the soil is a sprawling bed of ancient, molten lava, a form of rock.

West of the Cascades, the state is known for its rain and moderate climate. There, it gets more than 60 inches (152 cm) of rain per year. One town, Quillayute, is cloudy two-thirds of the year. But east of the Cascades, the state receives only a tenth of that amount of rain. Winters in the east are bitter, and summers hot and dry.

Puget Sound is the long, island-filled bay that extends 80 miles (129 km) southward through the state from Admiralty Inlet on the Pacific coast. Most of the major cities, including Seattle, Tacoma, Bremerton, and Olympia, are on Puget Sound. More than half the people in Washington State live in the vicinity of the sound. The San Juan Islands, an archipelago in the northern section of it, include more than 170 islands.

Washington has almost 160 miles (257 km) of coastline. The Pacific Ocean has been a key influence on the state's people and development for centuries. Today, it brings international shipping through the Strait of Juan de Fuca to ports in Washington and British Columbia. It is important not only for shipping and fishing but also for tourism. Visitors are especially eager to spy pods (groups) of killer whales just offshore.

Natural Beauty, Riches—and Challenges

Forests thick with fir and hemlock trees dominate the western part of the state. Washington is known as the Evergreen State. The

A Roosevelt elk grazes casually in Olympic National Park. The Olympic Peninsula is among America's most scenic and fascinating natural areas.

protected rain forest on the Olympic Peninsula contains trees as tall as 300 feet (91 m). Besides fir and hemlock, the rain forest contains many old cedar and spruce trees.

Eastern Washington is mainly farmland and prairie between the Cascade and Rocky Mountain ranges. Mineral deposits inside the earth include sand, gravel, zinc, lead, and olivine. Above, roaming and homing wild animals vary from coyotes to elk to mountain lions to bald eagles. Salmon, trout, and other fish thrive in the rivers.

From its steep and snowy mountains to its clear lakes and rushing rivers to its coast, Washington is quite a beautiful state. No wonder its leaders have set aside 262,000 acres (106,073 hectares) of state park land.

Environmentalists worry that human progress and steady growth are damaging the state's natural resources. They point to overfishing in the rivers and along the coast, and clear-cutting in the forests. They note lower river levels as a result of irrigation. Industries, in Washington as elsewhere, have polluted the environment. Wildlife has suffered. Endangered species in Washington already include the grizzly bear and peregrine falcon.

The attempt to balance progress with preservation is a major challenge everywhere. In Washington, with its growing population and many natural treasures, it is especially important.

An Odd Tale of Two Cities

Seattle is Washington's largest and most famous city—but it is not the state capital. Olympia, a city that many outsiders have never heard of, is the capital. The tale of how history reversed the importance of these two cities over time is interesting.

At the southern tip of Puget Sound, Olympia was founded near the site of the state's first pioneer settlement. Olympia is named for the nearby Olympic Mountains. (In ancient times, Olympia was a prominent city in Greece.) It became the capital when Washington was made a state in 1889.

Seattle, midway down the sound, is named for a Native chief who helped the early settlers. It grew faster than Olympia during the late 1800s. It was selected as the terminus, or end of the line, by two east-to-west railroad companies. During the twentieth century, it became the leading business and cultural center not just of Washington but of the whole Pacific Northwest.

As seen through the openings of a modern sculpture, downtown Seattle presents a striking skyline. The Space Needle, not surprisingly, dominates.

Seattle became even more famous when the World's Fair was held there in 1962. To emphasize the occasion, the city built its astonishing Space Needle. This is a slender, 605-foot (184-meter) skyscraper that features a revolving restaurant (called SkyCity) near the top. At the same time, Seattle also constructed the first monorail train in the United States.

Sports fans know a lot about Seattle. It is the home of the Seahawks (professional football), Mariners (professional baseball), and Storm (professional women's basketball). It has minor league teams in ice hockey, soccer, and other sports.

Olympia has no big-league sports organizations or world-famous buildings. Several other Washington cities besides Seattle have more citizens than Olympia. However, Olympia is a large city, home to almost fifty thousand residents. Most important, it is the center of government, the place where Washington's laws are made.

Chapter 2

The History of Washington

Before Europeans and Asians arrived, dozens of American Indian tribes occupied the land that is now Washington. Those who lived along the Pacific coast and what is now called Puget Sound in the western part of the state included the Chinook, Puyallup, Quinault, Nooksak, Skagit, Makah, Skokomish, Snohomish, and other Native groups. East of the Cascade Range, tribes included the Nez Percé, Okanogan, Spokane, Cayuse, Walla Walla, and Yakama (or Yakima).

The Chinook people were among the most prominent. They lived around the Columbia River. The Chinook were traders who developed a type of language with which they could communicate with other groups of people.

For food, the coastal people mainly fished and killed whales, seals, sea lions, and other sea creatures. The Makah were especially good at whaling. They used the meat for food and the blubber for fuel.

Coastal tribes were expert boat builders. Using stone tools and fire, they carved seaworthy canoes from giant tree trunks. Some were as long as 60 feet (18 m) and could carry more than a dozen whale hunters. Boat travel made it easier for the coastal groups to visit and trade with one another.

The people inhabiting the eastern part of the state were hunters, foragers, and river fishers. They killed deer, elk, and other wild game

An American artist in the late 1700s made this print of a spacious Chinook lodge. The central feature is a fire pit. Native peoples adapted efficiently to the weather.

of the forests and the Columbia Plateau. Interestingly, some of them made their homes by digging big holes and covering them with tree limbs and sod—unique, cozy, inexpensive, and easy-to-build houses.

Newcomers Arrive by Sea and Overland

Seafaring explorers from England and Spain touched at the coast of what is now Washington State during the eighteenth century. They traded for furs with the natives and mapped the coastline for those to come.

James Cook, one of the most famous English sea captains, arrived in 1778. The Columbia River is named for the ship commanded by Captain Robert Gray, who explored the area in 1792. Another noted explorer was George Vancouver. He probed the west coast of the area for almost three years, beginning in 1792.

The U.S. government became very interested

Fort Okanogan is pictured here as it appeared in the 1850s. Established in 1811, it was Washington State's first European settlement.

in the territory because of its fur resources. President Thomas Jefferson in 1804 sent explorers Meriwether Lewis and William Clark to map the Pacific Northwest. Their findings during the next two years helped land seekers from the East find their way into what are now the northwestern states. Soon after their expedition, forts and trading posts were set up in the Washington wilderness. The first settlement was Fort Okanogan, established in 1811.

England in those years was not ready to grant control of the Northwest to the upstart nation, the United States. Its great trading organization, the Hudson's Bay Company, founded Fort Vancouver on the Columbia River in 1825. Not until 1846 did England and the United States separate the region into U.S.-controlled Washington Territory (officially named that in 1853) and English-controlled British Columbia.

The "Good Life"

Coffee? Tourism? Computers? Young American Indians who inhabited what is now Washington State would have been astonished by the way many modern-day Washingtonians earn their living and enjoy their lives. In their day, people lived by hunting, fishing, farming, and trading with other tribes. It was a good life. Nightly storytelling in their primitive but warm dwellings, daily instruction by their parents in the ways of the forest—those were the good times they remembered.

They would have been confused by what modern Americans think is the "good life": working regular hours in an office, shop, or factory; meeting friends at restaurants and concerts; hiking, biking, and inline skating for pleasure; and communicating with strangers all over the world on a computer keyboard.

Washington's city skyscrapers would have astonished them, too. Their own villages, constructed of naturally available materials, were all they needed or wanted.

The United States steadily spread westward. Ships and wagon trains brought settlers, gold diggers, and adventurers into the California and Pacific Northwest coastal territories during the mid-1800s. In the 1860s and 1870s, railroads linked the East to the West with safer, faster overland travel. Until they did, travel across America into Washington took a long time. It was very hard and very dangerous. Westbound settlers were blocked by the extreme mountain ranges, deep and unpredictable rivers, and American Indians who did not completely welcome their arrival. One of the most shocking intercultural tragedies was the slaying of missionaries Marcus and Narcissa Whitman and other settlers in 1847.

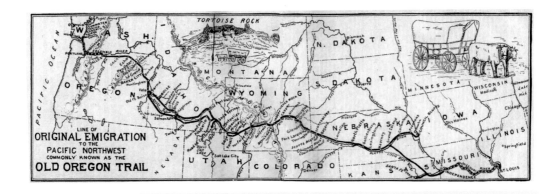

The famous Oregon Trail brought countless pioneers from the East to the Pacific Northwest during the 1800s. The founders of Seattle arrived by this route in 1851.

Many of the overland settlers came by the Oregon Trail. Among the first of them were Arthur and David Denny from New York. Arriving with others in 1851, they settled in what is now the Seattle area of Puget Sound. The Dennys were optimistic. They believed their frontier city would blossom and "pretty soon" would become the West Coast version of New York. They called their settlement Alki-New York. *Alki* is a Chinook word meaning "soon" or "in time."

The U.S. government wanted easterners to settle the northwestern territory. The government gave away land to white settlers—depriving the Indians of their home territories. Throughout the 1800s, the government made treaties with many tribes. Politicians wanted the tribes to move peacefully onto reservations. Time after time, however, white settlers, soldiers, miners, and government agents broke treaty terms. In many instances, the Indians rebelled. One such event in Washington Territory was the Yakima War (1855–1857).

Construction workers for the Northern Pacific Railroad take time from their labors to pose for a photographer. Note the Chinese laborer seated at left.

Marks of Progress:
Railroads, Cities, Dams

White settlers were amazed by the towering forests, sheer mountain faces, rushing rivers, and other natural wonders of the region. They established logging and lumber operations. Many of Washington's towns began as sawmill communities.

To this day, timber remains a big part of Washington's economy. New enterprises and interests quickly developed, though. The Northern Pacific Railway from Minnesota to the Washington coast was completed in 1883. It brought many more settlers into the territory.

Seattle's rapid growth suffered a great blow in June 1889. A fire broke out in a paint store and spread to destroy sixty downtown blocks. Determined citizens rebuilt Seattle and made it safer. Many of the original wooden buildings were replaced with brick and stone structures. By 1900, Seattle was one of the busiest ports on the Pacific coast. It was also becoming a shipbuilding center.

Washington became the forty-second state of the Union on November 11, 1889. Easterners and national leaders recognized it for its beauty and its enormous natural strengths. One famous symbol of that recognition is the Grand Coulee Dam. The largest concrete dam in the United States, it went under construction in 1934 during the Great Depression and was finished in 1942. It is on the Columbia River, spanning the state's border with Oregon.

Asians Add to the Mix— and Encounter Conflict

Many Asians, especially those of Japanese and Chinese descent, came to the U.S. West Coast during the nineteenth and twentieth centuries. They became a substantial part of the Pacific Northwest's varied cultural blend.

During World War II (1939–1945), when America and Japan fought against each other, thousands of Japanese Americans were placed in remote internment camps. Although they were not treated as harshly as prison inmates, they did lose most of their freedoms. The U.S. government was afraid Japanese Americans would try to help Japan in the war by spying or creating violent uprisings.

Today, Washington State has a rich culture with American Indian, European, Asian, and other influences.

Chapter 3

THE GOVERNMENT OF WASHINGTON

Washington has thirty-nine counties and numerous cities and towns. Each town, city, and county has its own system of local government. Local elected and appointed leaders form policies. City and county government workers in many offices enforce laws and provide the services that citizens pay for with their local taxes. City and district courts handle legal disputes and try criminal cases.

On a larger scale, the state government is based on the constitution that was drafted in 1878, before Washington earned statehood. The constitution has been changed by amendments throughout the years.

The governor heads the executive branch of the state government. The lieutenant governor has special duties and is the person who will take charge if the governor dies or becomes unable to serve. Both officials are elected by Washington voters. Other leaders, including the secretary of state, attorney general, auditor, and superintendent of public instruction, are also elected. These executives oversee the performance of state government agencies and services, and decide how tax money will be used.

It's interesting to note that Washington citizens don't pay state taxes on their normal incomes. (They must pay federal taxes on income, like citizens in other states.) The state relies primarily on sales taxes—taxes on purchases—to support government programs.

Washington's legislative branch of government consists of a state senate and house of representatives. Washington has forty-nine state senators and ninety-eight state representatives, all of them elected. As in many other states, senators in Washington are elected for four-year terms. House members serve two-year terms. The main duty of a legislature is fairly simple: to make laws. New laws must constantly be made as new problems arise and older, unsolved problems become more and more serious.

The state's judicial branch of government is in charge of all court matters. Most legal issues, from property disputes to certain

Gardens surround Washington's state capitol building in Olympia. Though not as well known as Seattle, Olympia is the seat of state government.

types of crime, are handled in municipal (city) courts. Some cases go before one of Washington's twenty-nine higher state courts, called superior courts. Washington also has a court of appeals to resolve disputed lower court decisions. At the top of the judicial branch is the Washington Supreme Court.

Withstanding Nature

It took six years to finish the current Washington State legislative building, completed in 1922. New York architects Harry White and Walter Wilder designed the structure some years earlier, but World War I (1914–1918) and other events interfered.

Perhaps its most interesting aspect is its ability to withstand the natural challenges of the Pacific Northwest. Earthquakes are common. Three major ones shook the area in 1949, 1965, and 2001. After each calamity, city leaders and engineers bolstered the structure. In the aftermath of the 2001 alarm, they spent $120 million in a three-year project to improve plumbing, heating, cooling, technology, and other factors that can affect citizens in the event of such a catastrophe. They also turned their attention to recycling and solar paneling. The 144 solar panels placed on the roof of the legislative building represent the greatest solar panel installation among all the U.S. state capitols.

This 1913 drawing gives a good idea of what the new state government building in Olympia would look like.

These three government branches—executive, legislative, and judicial—work together in a system of checks and balances, which is the basis of U.S. government. The nation's founders did not want any single branch of government to attain too much power. For example, the governor appoints judges, but the legislature must approve the appointments. Members of the legislature also have the power to question the operations of executive agencies. Members of the state supreme court serve only six-year terms—unlike the U.S. Supreme Court, where appointments are permanent.

Notable Washington Leaders

Washington has established itself as a progressive state in its selection of leaders. One of its first governors, John Rankin Rogers, was a farmer and businessman who was elected as a Populist candidate in 1896. He championed farm causes and public education.

Dixy Lee Ray became Washington's first woman governor in 1976. Before being elected, she chaired the U.S. Atomic Energy Commission.

Dixy Lee Ray, a native of Tacoma, was the state's first female governor, serving from 1977 to 1981. A scientist by profession, Ray also chaired the U.S. Atomic Energy Commission.

Gary Locke became the first Asian American governor in the continental United States in 1996. Locke served two four-year terms.

Governor Christine Gregoire took office in January 2005 and was reelected in 2008.

Prominent Washingtonians in national politics include Thomas S. Foley. He served in Congress from 1965 to 1995, and during his last six years in office he was Speaker of the House. Foley then served as ambassador to Japan from 1997 to 2001.

Warren G. Magnuson was the state's longest-serving U.S. senator, holding office from 1944 to 1980. Magnuson is remembered for his work to protect consumer interests and the environment. Another Washingtonian, Henry M. "Scoop" Jackson, served in the U.S. Senate from 1952 to 1983.

Washington's first congresswoman was Catherine May, who served from 1958 until 1970. May was formerly an English teacher and radio announcer. In Congress, she served on the Agriculture Committee and the House-Senate Atomic Energy Committee. She cosponsored the 1963 Equal Pay Act and was an early supporter of the Equal Rights Amendment.

Washington was also the home state of U.S. Supreme Court justice William O. Douglas. Appointed in 1939, he served on the Court until 1975—longer than any other justice.

Chapter 4

THE ECONOMY OF WASHINGTON

A hundred years ago, two-thirds of Washington State's labor force worked in the timber industry. People at the time did not even dream of airplanes and computers—the foundations of two of the state's most vibrant modern industries. Timber remains important, but the state's economy today is very healthy because it is so diverse.

Trees, Farms, Ships, and Factories

Timber, or forestry, includes the production of lumber (boards for building) and paper, which is made of wood. Washington is the second-ranking lumber-producing state in the nation. It also turns out great quantities of plywood, a soft wood compound.

Washington farmers are known for their apples, wheat, potatoes, hay, and other fruits and vegetables. They harvest as many as ten billion apples a year. Washington is the country's leading apple-producing state. It is famous for its Red Delicious apples. Washington also has many greenhouses that produce flowers and herbs.

The Tri-Cities metropolis—Kennewick, Pasco, and Richland/West Richland—is in south-central Washington. Known especially for its surrounding farms, the Tri-Cities is one of the leading wine-producing areas of the country. The Yakima Valley, upriver from the Tri-Cities,

Apple Capital

The climate and geography of central and eastern Washington are perfect for growing apples. The soil contains lava ash and other beneficial minerals, and the air is dry much of the year. Insects are not a serious problem for farmers, and there is lots of sunshine. Central Washington has more than 175,000 acres (71 hectares) of orchards and ships roughly one hundred million boxes of fresh apples each year worldwide. During harvest time in September and October, some forty thousand apple pickers are at work.

Apple growing began with early settlers in the 1820s. By 1890, growers were beginning to sell their fruit far and wide. Washington was the first state to grade its apples, letting buyers know the levels of quality. For almost a century now, Washington has been America's leading apple-producing state.

People in Wenatchee call their city the "Apple Capital of the World." Wenatchee, situated directly in the middle of the state on the Columbia River, is the home of the Washington Apple Commission's Visitors Center.

Workers cull out lower-grade apples at a packing plant in Wenatchee. Washington prides itself not only for its high-volume apple production but also for the fruit's quality.

is a leading international producer of hops, an ingredient of beer and other alcoholic beverages.

Livestock farming and the production of dairy products are important to the state's economy. So are its fisheries. As you would expect, the fishing industry is centered in Puget Sound and along the coast. From Washington's rivers come salmon, popular nationwide.

An underwater net system rigged between two boats catches salmon. This technique, reef net fishing, was developed by Native Americans.

Shipbuilding has provided an important livelihood for generations of Washingtonians. The state is also an international port of call. Although far inland from the Pacific Ocean, Seattle is one of the nation's five largest container ports.

Washington's factories produce machinery, electronic equipment, metalwork, clothes, and processed foods. Most factories operate around Puget Sound.

Airplanes and Computers

Besides the kinds of factories found elsewhere around the country, modern industries also thrive in Washington State. Two of the most significant are aeronautics and computer technology.

The Boeing Company continues to produce new aircraft after almost a century. Shown here is the first flight of a gigantic Boeing 777 Freighter.

William E. Boeing was born in Detroit, Michigan. He dropped out of Yale University in 1903 and moved to Washington to begin logging on property owned by the family. Soon afterward, he became fascinated with airplanes and learned to fly them—and build them. The Boeing Company has been making commercial and military airliners and other aircraft for almost a century.

Boeing founded his airplane factory in Seattle in 1916. By the end of World War I, the Boeing Airplane Company was building planes for the U.S. Navy. The company became a world leader in aeronautics during World War II, when it built thousands of huge bombers for the U.S. armed forces. As the world progressed into the space age, so did Boeing.

The nation's economy constantly goes up and down. Just as Washingtonians have enjoyed happy years because of their state's major industries, they have suffered when the industries have suffered. In 1969, for example, Boeing had to lay off more than half of its workers. That was because the need for new aircraft had dwindled. Thousands of Seattle-area residents lost their jobs.

Perhaps Washington State's biggest business success story is Microsoft. College students started the company as a "garage" enterprise.

But the Boeing Company continues to be a major employer in Washington State. It moved its headquarters to Chicago, Illinois, in 2001. However, several of its facilities and almost half of its 163,000 employees remain in Washington.

An even greater Washington success story came later. During the mid-1970s, while still college students, Seattle natives Bill Gates and Paul Allen started a small software company, Microsoft. When personal computers (PCs) became popular several years later, Microsoft became the leading provider of PC operating systems. Microsoft Corporation, based in Redmond, is today worth more than half a trillion dollars. That's more money than the entire United States has in circulation. Because of Microsoft, other technology companies are headquartered nearby, employing additional computer professionals. Companies all over the world work closely with Microsoft in developing computer software and hardware.

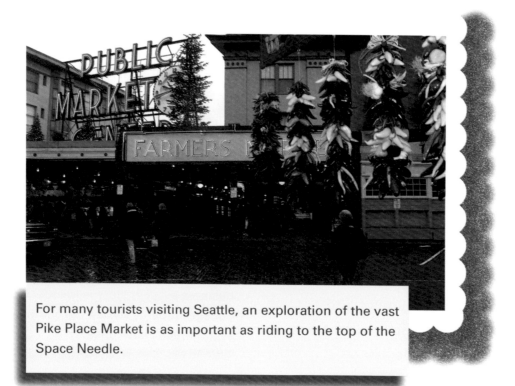

For many tourists visiting Seattle, an exploration of the vast Pike Place Market is as important as riding to the top of the Space Needle.

Serving Society

Most Washingtonians work in the service sector. They include health care and educational professionals, restaurant and lodging employees, tourism specialists, and other workers who are hired to provide various services to society.

Tourism is especially big business. Seattle is a popular destination in itself, noted for its dining, sports, and cultural events. The Space Needle is a must-visit, and a trip to Seattle is incomplete without exploring the sprawling Pike Place Market on Puget Sound.

Tourists also come to enjoy the state's great outdoors. They climb mountains, hike, camp, ski, fish, look for whales along the coast, and go biking and boating. Some tourists take helicopter flights over the top of Mount Saint Helens, the site of the horrific volcano eruption in 1980.

Chapter 5

PEOPLE FROM WASHINGTON: PAST AND PRESENT

The people of Washington represent practically every part of the United States—and many foreign countries. Many American Indian, European, and Asian cultural backgrounds form a rich, colorful human tapestry.

Not surprisingly, numerous festivals take place each year around the state. Some feature Native American culture. Some are devoted to the customs of European and Asian ethnic groups. Others focus on different arts.

Here is a small sampling of people who made—and continue to make—Washington such an interesting state.

Chief Seattle (Seatlh) (1790–1866) Chief Seattle was born near Puget Sound. He became the leader of the Suquamish and other tribes. In 1855, he signed a major treaty with the European settlers. He died on a reservation in 1866.

Mary Richardson Walker (1811–1897) Mary Richardson Walker and her husband, Elkanah, were missionaries to the Spokane Indians during the mid-1800s. While crossing America from east to west, she wrote a long, fascinating diary telling of their struggle to survive and of the Indians and

Native Cultures

American Indian heritage is found throughout Washington State. Native cultures are sparse and isolated in some states, especially in the East. But in the West, they are quite prominent.

Washington State has twenty-seven American Indian reservations. They are home to people from many tribes with differing languages and cultures. Museums around the state contain Native American artifacts. On certain reservations, larger facilities are devoted to native life and history. One is the Yakama Nation Cultural Heritage Center in Toppenish, inside the Yakama Indian Reservation. The building looks much like a Yakama winter lodge of old. Besides examining the displays, visitors can conduct research in the center's special library and buy handmade crafts in the gift shop. They can even sample traditional Yakama food, such as fry bread and salmon stew, at the Heritage Inn Restaurant.

Another interesting place is the Lelooska Foundation in Ariel. It show-cases Native American arts. On certain weekends, visitors can hear tribal story-tellers and see exciting masked dances.

All Washingtonians can take special pride in this aspect of their state's historical preservation.

This photograph of Chief Seattle was taken around 1865. As a leader of combined Native peoples, he signed a treaty in 1855 that was important for European settlers.

traders they met. Historians consider it a priceless document because of its honesty and detail.

Isaac Stevens (1818–1862) President Franklin Pierce appointed Isaac Stevens the first governor of Washington Territory in 1853. He was a veteran soldier and surveyor. During his four years in office, he pushed for a railroad route through the rugged mountains. He also negotiated treaties with Indian tribes. Stevens was killed during the Civil War in 1862, serving as a brigadier general in the Union army.

Bertha Knight Landes (1868–1943) She was the first woman to be elected mayor of a major U.S. city when she won the Seattle mayor's race in 1926. This was in an era when few women held any type of public office.

Eddie Bauer (1899–1986) Eddie Bauer, famous for his brand-name outdoor clothing line, was a native of Orcas Island in Puget Sound. He became interested in developing high-quality outerwear after almost freezing to death while on a fishing trip in 1923.

Bertha Knight Landes, Seattle's first woman mayor, meets explorer Roald Amundsen in 1926.

Nora B. Adams (1929–2004) Nora B. Adams was an African American school principal in

Seattle. Although highly respected as an educator, she is remembered even more for her monetary contributions to education and health research. A wise investor, Adams donated more than $1 million to scholarships and medical science.

Bonnie J. Dunbar flew aboard the space shuttle in the 1980s and 1990s.

Dick Scobee (1939–1986), Richard Gordon Jr. (1929–), Bonnie J. Dunbar (1949–), and Michael P. Anderson (1959–2003) Washington's contributions to aeronautics include the work of several astronauts. Dick Scobee, born in Cle Elum, died aboard the space shuttle *Challenger* when it exploded in 1986. Richard Gordon Jr., a Seattle native, was one of the first astronauts to reach the moon as an *Apollo XII* crew member in 1969. Bonnie J. Dunbar, of Sunnyside, made five space shuttle flights. Michael P. Anderson, a New York native who grew up in Spokane, died in the space shuttle *Columbia* disaster in 2003.

Lee Orr (1917–) Among the state's best-known athletes is Lee Orr. A track and football star during the 1930s, he set state records and competed in the 1936 Olympics. Although he did not win, he tied the world record for the 200-meter dash in the quarterfinal Olympic run.

Bing Crosby (1903–1977) Born in Tacoma, Harry Lillis "Bing" Crosby was a movie and recording star throughout the mid-1900s. He recorded more songs than any other singer, had more than twenty gold records, and was featured in some four thousand radio broadcasts. He also performed in fifty-five films. Crosby raised millions of dollars in war bonds during World War II and founded a celebrity golf tournament to benefit charity.

Jimi Hendrix (1942–1970) Jimi Hendrix was a famous rock guitarist during the 1960s. Although he could not read music, he was considered a musical genius because of his talent, creativity, and exploration of the instrument. Born in Seattle, Hendrix died at age twenty-seven.

Pearl Jam Pearl Jam is a popular Seattle-based rock band. It was formed in 1990 as Mookie Blaylock and changed its name the next year. Since then, the band has sold more than sixty million recordings.

Dale Chihuly (1941–) One of Washington's most famous artists is Dale Chihuly, a glass blower. Born in Tacoma, Chihuly cofounded Pilchuk, a world-renowned glass-blowing school, in the northwestern part of the state in 1971. Chihuly has succeeded despite partial blindness and other injuries suffered in a 1976 auto accident.

George Tsutakawa (1910–1997) Another famous artisan was George Tsutakawa. A Japanese American born in Seattle, he designed more than seventy public fountains. Tsutakawa

Sculptor, painter, and architect George Tsutakawa designed this fantastic bronze fountain on the waterfront of his native Seattle.

was also a painter and sculptor. He taught art and architecture for more than thirty years at the University of Washington.

Minoru Yamasaki (1912– 1986) This Seattle native earned fame as a different kind of architect. Yamasaki designed the World Trade Center in New York City— the tallest buildings in the world when they were finished in 1976. He died fifteen years before his masterpiece was destroyed by terrorists on September 11, 2001.

Norman B. Rice (1943–) Norman B. Rice served as Seattle's first black mayor from 1990 to 1997. His election was considered remarkable because of Seattle's low percentage of African American citizens (fewer than 10 percent). Rice is noted for his work toward educational improvement and business development during his two terms in office.

From the people and lifestyles of early Native Americans to the computer and aerospace technology of the twenty-first century, Washington is unique. It is a state rich in diversity and blessed with natural beauty. And it is a wonderful place to live or to visit.

Timeline

20,000 BCE	American Indian groups begin to occupy the area.
1592	Spanish explorers arrive.
1778	English explorer James Cook visits the area; other explorers follow.
1805	The Lewis and Clark overland expedition arrives at the Pacific Ocean after crossing North America.
1811	The first settlement is established at Fort Okanogan.
1836	Missionaries come to Walla Walla Valley.
1860	Gold and silver strikes are made.
1861	The University of Washington is founded.
1889	Seattle is ravaged by fire but is rebuilt; the same year, Washington becomes a state.
1897	The Klondike gold rush in Alaska makes Seattle a more prosperous transportation center.
1916	Aviation pioneer William Boeing flies his first plane.
1942	Construction of the Grand Coulee Dam across the Columbia River is done.
1962	The World's Fair opens in Seattle.
1971	Starbucks Coffee Company is established. Starbucks will eventually open more than fifteen thousand shops worldwide.
1975	Microsoft Corporation is founded.
1980	Mount Saint Helens erupts.
2001	A major earthquake strikes the Seattle area.
2006	A December windstorm kills fourteen people and leaves millions without electrical power in western Washington State.
2008	The Seattle Supersonics professional basketball team relocates to Oklahoma City.

State motto	*Alki*, a Chinook word that means "in time." (Settlers at what is now Alki Point named the place Alki-New York. They wanted it to become a grand city like New York, "in time.")
State capital	Olympia
State flower	Coast rhododendron
State bird	Willow goldfinch
State tree	Western hemlock
State fruit	Apple
Year of statehood	1889, forty-second state admitted to the Union
State nickname	Evergreen State
Total area and U.S. rank	66,582 square miles (172,448 square km), eighteenth-largest state
Approximate population	Six million, fifteenth-most-populated state
Length of coastline	160 miles (257 km)
Highest and lowest elevations	14,410 feet (4,392 m) at Mount Rainier, zero feet (sea level) at Pacific coast

State Flag

State Seal

Major rivers and water bodies	Columbia River, Snake River, Yakima River, Puget Sound
Hottest and coldest temperatures	118 degrees Fahrenheit (48 degrees Celsius), August 5, 1961; -48°F (-44°C), December 30, 1968
Origin of state name	George Washington, first president of the United States
Chief agricultural products	Apples, wheat, potatoes, livestock
Major industries	Timber, electronics, aeronautics, tourism, shipbuilding

State Bird

State Flower

GLOSSARY

aeronautics Having to do with airplanes and spacecraft.

amendment A change made to a state constitution, usually after prolonged debate and public vote.

attorney general A state's official lawyer; this person advises governing officials about public legal issues.

clear-cutting The entire removal of a stand of timber, leaving barren landscape exposed.

environmentalist A person who is concerned about protecting natural habitats and resources.

executive branch The governor and other state administrative officers, some of them elected and some appointed by the governor; they are responsible for seeing that the state government and all its agencies operate effectively.

hardware The physical structure and attachments of a computer.

irrigation The diverting of water from lakes and streams onto farm crops during the growing season.

judicial branch The government's court system, which interprets a state's laws and executes justice.

lava Hot, liquid matter that gushes to the surface from volcanoes and cools into rock form.

legislative branch The lawmaking branch of state government, consisting of elected members of the state senate and state house of representatives.

monorail A single railway track, rather than two parallel tracks.

operating system The software that determines how a computer will function with all other software.

plateau A sprawling, mostly flat surface of land.

Populist A U.S. political party of the 1890s that appealed especially to farmers and other working-class voters.

preservation The saving of buildings and natural resources that are in danger of being lost to modern development and to the ravages of time and weather.

rain shadow effect The effect caused when air rises up the windward side of a mountain and the moisture is squeezed out. As the air descends the leeward side of the mountain, it dries, then warms and expands, therefore reducing the chance of precipitation.

software A computer program designed to perform a specific function, such as word processing, math calculation, or management of information files.

war bond A type of investment citizens made in the U.S. government during World War II to support military efforts.

FOR MORE INFORMATION

City of Seattle

600 Fourth Avenue

Seattle, WA 98124

(206) 684-2489

Web site: http://www.seattle.gov

The city of Seattle's government headquarters provides a variety of information at its Web site.

City of Wenatchee

P.O. Box 519

Wenatchee, WA 98807

(509) 888-6200

Web site: http://www.wenatcheewa.gov

This is the city government headquarters of the "Apple Capital of the World."

Department of Archaeology and Historic Preservation

1063 South Capitol Way, Suite 106

Olympia, WA 98501

(360) 586-3065

Web site: http://www.dahp.wa.gov

The department provides resources for researchers of the state's past.

History Ink/HistoryLink

1411 Fourth Avenue

Seattle, WA 98101

(206) 447-8140

Web site: http://www.historylink.org

HistoryLink.org is a free online encyclopedia devoted to Washington State history.

Office of the Governor

P.O. Box 40002

Olympia, WA 98504-0002

(360) 902-4111

Web site: http://www.governor.wa.gov

The Web site provides information on the governor's cabinet and department activities.

Olympia-Lacey-Tumwater Visitor and Convention Bureau

The Business Center

809 Legion Way SE

Olympia, WA 98501

(360) 704-7544

(877) 704-7500

Web site: http://www.visitolympia.com

This bureau provides information for visitors to the Washington State capital and nearby cities.

Tri-Cities Visitor and Convention Bureau

P.O. Box 2241

Tri-Cities, WA 99302-2241

(800) 254-5824

(509) 735-8486

Web site: http://www.visittri-cities.com

This bureau promotes the southern Washington cities of Kennewick, Pasco, and Richland/ West Richland.

Washington State Department of Community, Trade, and Economic Development

P.O. Box 42525

Olympia, WA 98504-2525

(360) 725-4000

Web site: http://cted.wa.gov

This department oversees community services, housing, local government, trade and economic development, public works, and state energy policies.

Web Sites

Due to the changing nature of Internet links, Rosen Publishing has developed an online list of Web sites related to the subject of this book. This site is updated regularly. Please use this link to access the list:

http://www.rosenlinks.com/uspp/wapp

FOR FURTHER READING

Covert, Kim. *Washington* (Land of Liberty). Mankato, MN: Capstone Press, 2004.

Davis, Jeff, and Al Eufrasio. *Weird Washington: Your Travel Guide to Washington's Local Legends and Best Kept Secrets*. New York, NY: Sterling, 2008.

Washington: The Evergreen State (Discover America). Chicago, IL: Encyclopedia Britannica, 2005.

The Washington Almanac: Facts About Washington (State Almanac Series). Portland, OR: Westwinds Press, 2003.

Webster, Christine. *Washington* (From Sea to Shining Sea). New York, NY: Children's Press, 2003.

Williams, Hill. *The Restless Northwest: A Geologic Story*. Pullman, WA: Washington State University Press, 2002.

BIBLIOGRAPHY

Access Washington: Official State Government Web Site. "Government in Washington." Retrieved November 24, 2008 (http://access.wa.gov/government/index.aspx).

Access Washington: Official State Government Web Site. "State Facts." Retrieved November 30, 2008 (http://access.wa.gov/statefacts/index.aspx).

BingCrosby.com. Retrieved November 21, 2008 (http://www.bingcrosby.com).

Boeing. "Boeing Employment Numbers." Retrieved December 1, 2008 (http://www.boeing.com/employment/employment_table.html).

Boeing. "William E. Boeing." Retrieved December 1, 2008 (http://www.boeing.com/history/boeing/boeing.html).

General Administration, State of Washington. "Washington State Capitol Tour: The Grounds." Retrieved November 30, 2008 (http://www.ga.wa.gov/visitor/CapitolTour/grounds.htm).

HistoryLink.org. "Adams, Nora B.," "Anderson, Ernestine," "Bauer, Eddie," "Chihuly, Dale," "Douglas, William O.," "Hendrix, Jimi," "Magnuson, Warren G.," "Orr, Lee," "Rice, Norman B.," "Tsutakawa, George," "Walker, Mary Richardson," "Yamasaki, Minoru." Retrieved November 2008 (http://www.historylink.org).

Insight Guides. *Seattle City Guide*. 4th ed. London, England: Insight Guides, 2007.

Kirk, Ruth, and Carmela Alexander. *Exploring Washington's Past: A Road Guide to History.* Seattle, WA: University of Washington Press, 1990.

Krist, Gary. *The White Cascade: The Great Northern Railway Disaster and America's Deadliest Avalanche.* New York, NY: Henry Holt and Company, 2007.

National Aeronautics and Space Administration Biographical Data. "Bonnie J. Dunbar." Retrieved December 16, 2008 (http://www.jsc.nasa.gov/Bios/htmlbios/dunbar.html).

National Governors Association. "Washington Governor John Rankin Rogers." Retrieved November 25, 2008 (http://www.nga.org/portal/site/nga/menuitem.29fab9fb4add 37305ddcbeeb501010a0/?vgnextoid=d4e14a3ff3045010VgnVCM1000001a01010aRCRD).

Netstate. "The Geography of Washington." Retrieved November 18, 2008 (http://www. netstate.com/states/geography/wa_geography.htm).

Ohlsen, Becky. *Seattle City Guide.* Oakland, CA: Lonely Planet Publications, 2008.

Pearl Jam—Ten Club. "Pearl Jam." Retrieved November 24, 2008 (http://www. pearljam.com).

Samson, Karl. *Frommer's Seattle 2008.* Hoboken, NJ: Wiley, 2007.

INDEX

About the Author

Daniel E. Harmon is the author of more than sixty books and thousands of articles for national and regional magazines and newspapers. His geographical and historical books include a profile of the Hudson River, works on the exploration of America and other parts of the world, and international studies of numerous world nations.

Photo credits

Cover (top left) Library of Congress Prints and Photographs Division; cover (top right), pp. 3, 6, 15, 22, 27, 33, 39, 41 Wikimedia Commons; cover (bottom) Dan Callister/Getty Images; p. 4 (top) © GeoAtlas; p. 7 © www.istockphoto.com/Nathan Fabro; p. 8 Courtesy of the U.S. Geological Survey, Austin Post; p. 10 © Jim Richardson/Corbis; pp. 12, 14 Shutterstock.com; pp. 16, 20 MPI/Hulton Archive/Getty Images; pp. 17, 24, 34, 35 Washington State Historical Society, Tacoma; p. 19 Courtesy of the University of Texas Libraries, the University of Texas at Austin; p. 23 B. Anthony Stewart/National Geographic/Getty Images; p. 25 © Bettmann/Corbis; p. 28 Douglas Graham/Congressional Quarterly/Getty Images; p. 29 © Dan Lamont/Corbis; p. 30 Stephen Brashear/Getty Images; p. 31 Robert Giroux/Getty Images; p. 32 John G. Mabanglo/AFP/Getty Images; p. 36 NASA; p. 38 Jeffree Stewart; p. 40 (left) Courtesy of Robesus, Inc.

Designer: Les Kanturek; Editor: Kathy Kuhtz Campbell;
Photo Researcher: Cindy Reiman